T0397867

EVA LONGORIA

ACTOR AND SOCIAL ACTIVIST

by Rachel Rose

Consultant: Beth Gambro
Reading Specialist, Yorkville, Illinois

BEARPORT
PUBLISHING

Minneapolis, Minnesota

Teaching Tips

BEFORE READING

- Look at the cover of the book. Discuss the picture and the title.

- Ask readers to brainstorm a list of what they already know about Eva Longoria. What can they expect to see in this book?

- Go on a picture walk, looking through the pictures to discuss vocabulary and make predictions about the text.

DURING READING

- Read for purpose. Encourage readers to look for key pieces of information they can expect to see in biographies.

- Ask readers to look for the details of the book. What happened to Eva Longoria at different times of her life?

- If readers encounter an unknown word, ask them to look at the sounds in the word. Then, ask them to look at the rest of the page. Are there any clues to help them understand?

AFTER READING

- Encourage readers to pick a buddy and reread the book together.

- Ask readers to name three things Eva Longoria has done throughout her life. Go back and find the pages that tell about these things.

- Ask readers to write or draw something they learned about Eva Longoria.

Credits:
Cover and title page, ©Dominique Charriau/WireImage/Getty Images and Robert Daly/iStock; 3, ©Kathy Hutchins/Shutterstock; 5, ©Kathy Hutchins/Shutterstock; 7, ©Roschetzky Photography/Shutterstock; 8, ©Paya Mona/Shutterstock; 11, ©CBS Photo Archive Contributor/Getty Images; 13, ©Stephen Shugerman / Stringer/Getty Images; 15, ©MWA/ZOJ/Michael Wright/WENN/Newscom; 17, ©Owen Hoffmann / Stringer/Getty Images; 19, ©Edward A. Ornelas/ZUMAPRESS/Newscom/Newscom; 21, ©TinseltownShutterstock; 22, ©Kathy Hutchins/Shutterstock; 23, ©GONZALO/Bauer-Griffin/Contributor/Getty Images; 23, ©smutny pan/Shutterstock; 23, ©GaudiLab/Shutterstock; 23, ©Denis Kuvaev/Shutterstock; 23, ©Jemal Countess/StringerGetty Images; 23, ©Bob Pool/Shutterstock

Library of Congress Cataloging-in-Publication Data is available at www.loc.gov or upon request from the publisher.

ISBN: 978-1-63691-716-0 (hardcover)
ISBN: 978-1-63691-723-8 (paperback)
ISBN: 978-1-63691-730-6 (ebook)

For more information, write to Bearport Publishing, 5357 Penn Avenue South, Minneapolis, MN 55419. Printed in the United States of America.

Contents

Hollywood Star

Eva Longoria smiled for the **cameras**.

Click, click, click!

People cheered for her.

Eva was being **honored** for her **acting**.

Eva's Life

Long ago, Eva's family lived in Mexico.

But Eva grew up in Texas.

She calls herself Texican for being from both places.

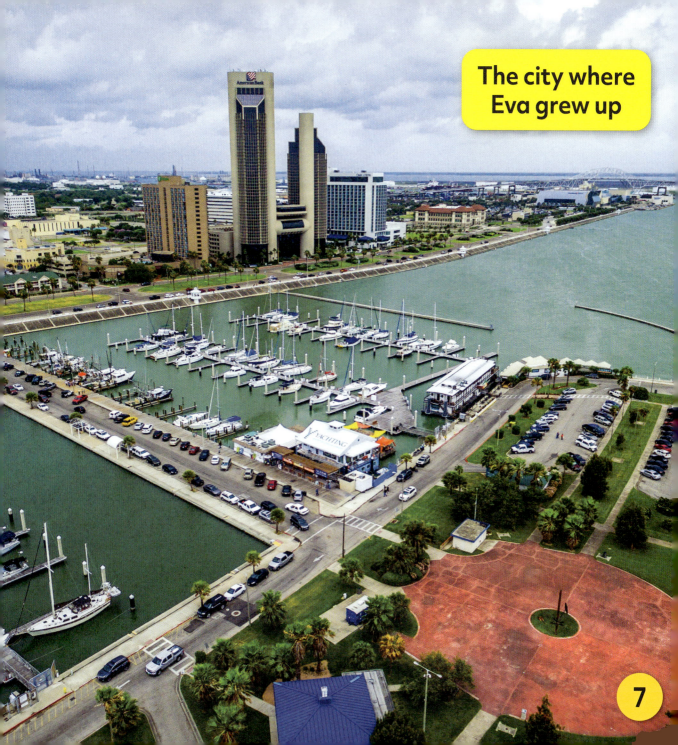

The city where Eva grew up

Eva's family lived on a **ranch**.

She spent a lot of time with her three older sisters.

Other people from her family lived nearby.

When she was older, Eva moved to California.

She started acting.

Eva worked hard to get jobs.

One of Eva's first big jobs was on a TV show.

She played a woman named Gabrielle.

Gabrielle was smart and funny just like Eva.

Eva with others from her show

Soon, Eva wanted to do more than act.

She started doing other TV jobs.

Sometimes, Eva was the one in charge.

15

But something bugged Eva.

She did not work with many people like her.

So, she started her own **company**.

Eva wants more kinds of people to help make shows.

17

Even outside of work, Eva helps people.

She started a group for people with **disabilities**.

It is called Eva's Heroes.

THE TEXAS CAVALIERS CHARITABLE FOUNDATION
SAN ANTONIO, TEXAS

APRIL 11, 2011   040711

EVA'S HEROES

FIFTY THOUSAND DOLLARS $ 50,000.00

                                                              Dollars

THE TEXAS CAVALIERS CHARITABLE FOUNDATION
DONATION HONORING EVA'S HEROES

Memo

123 45678 9012 345

Jorge Canseco
JORGE CANSECO
PRESIDENT, TEXAS CAVALIERS CHARITABLE FOUNDATION 2010-2011

19

Eva is very busy.

She acts and she has many other jobs.

She helps as many people as she can.

That's what she cares about the most.

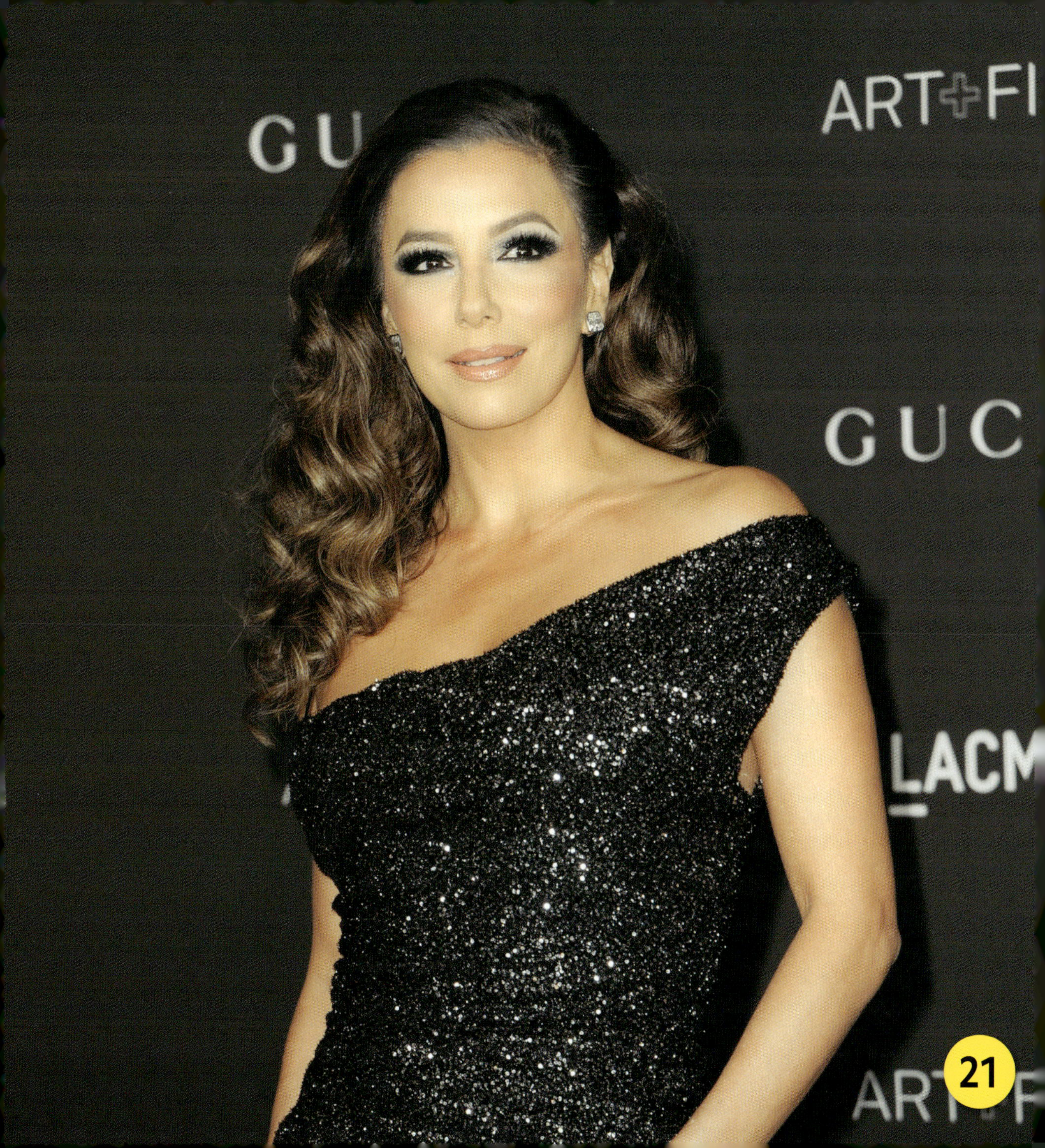
GUC
ART+FI
GUC
LACM
ART+FI

Did You Know?

Born: March 15, 1975

Family: Ella Eva (mother), Enrique Jr. (father), Elizabeth (sister), Emily (sister), Esmerelda (sister)

When she was a kid: She worked at a restaurant. Eva wanted to make money to have a big birthday party.

Special fact: Her sister Elizabeth has a disability. Eva calls her sister her hero.

Eva says: "Whatever you want to do, just start."

Life Connections

Eva likes to learn how to do new things. Is there something you want to learn? What can you do to get better at something new?

Glossary

acting playing a part in a show or movie

cameras things that take pictures or videos

company a group or person that does a job

disabilities things that make it harder to learn things, do things, or deal with feelings

honored shown great respect

ranch a large farm with cows, horses, or sheep

Index

Read More

Alexander, Vincent. *Volunteering (Being an Active Citizen).* Minneapolis: Jump! 2019.

Keppeler, Jill. *Families with Special Needs (All Kinds of Families).* New York: PowerKids Press, 2021.

Learn More Online

1. Go to **www.factsurfer.com** or scan the QR code below.
2. Enter "**Eva Longoria**" into the search box.
3. Click on the cover of this book to see a list of websites.

About the Author

Rachel Rose is a writer who lives in California. Her favorite books to write are about people who lead inspiring lives.